TRUMPET

BEST of BEETHOVEN

TRUMPET

CONTENTS

Instrumental arrangements by David Pearl

Cherry Lane Music Company
Director of Publications: Mark Phillips
Publications Coordinator: Rebecca Skidmore

ISBN: 978-1-60378-267-8

Visit our website at www.cherrylaneprint.com

FÜR ELISE

TRUMPET

By Ludwig van Beethoven

Moderately

rit.

PIANO CONCERTO NO. 3
First Movement

TRUMPET

by Ludwig van Beethoven

Moderately, in 2

Orchestra

Play

PIANO SONATA NO. 14 "MOONLIGHT"

First Movement

TRACK 3

TRUMPET

By Ludwig van Beethoven

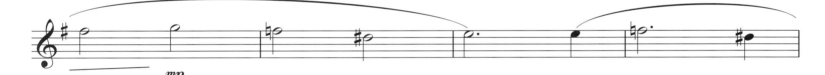

poco rit.   a tempo

rit.

PIANO TRIO NO. 7 "ARCHDUKE"

Third Movement

TRUMPET

By Ludwig van Beethoven

TRACK 5

SYMPHONY NO. 2
Second Movement

TRUMPET

By Ludwig van Beethoven

Moderately slow

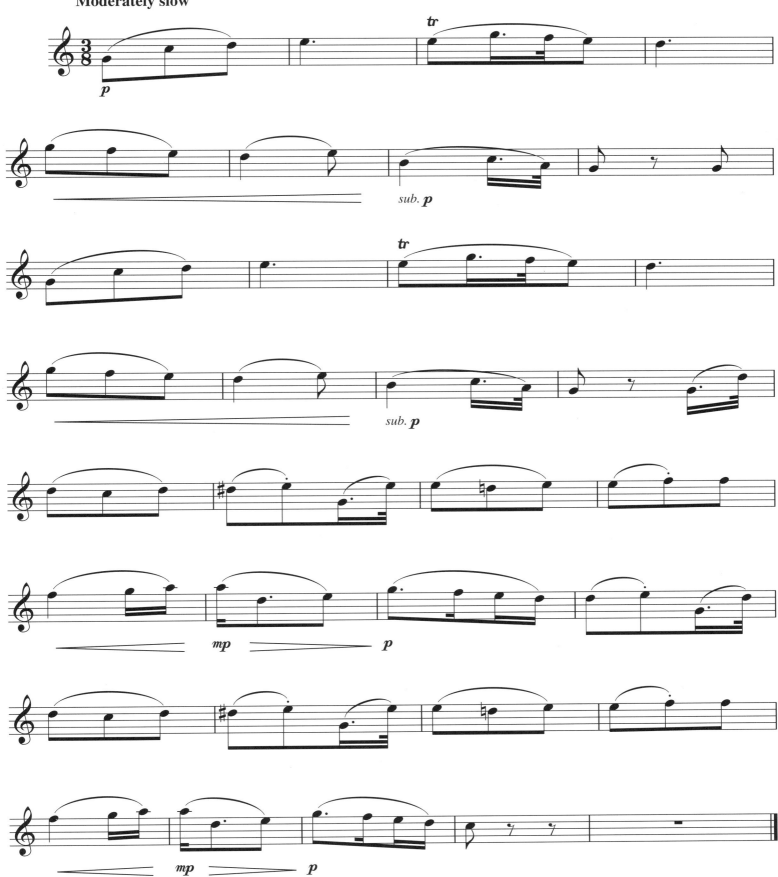

SYMPHONY NO. 3
Second Movement

TRUMPET

By Ludwig van Beethoven

Slowly

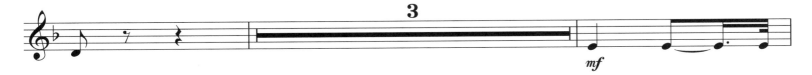

SYMPHONY NO. 5

First Movement

TRUMPET

By Ludwig van Beethoven

SYMPHONY NO. 6

Fifth Movement

TRUMPET

By Ludwig van Beethoven

SYMPHONY NO. 7
Second Movement

TRUMPET

By Ludwig van Beethoven

Moderately slow

Orchestra

Play

SYMPHONY NO. 8
Second Movement

TRUMPET

By Ludwig van Beethoven

Moderately

TURKISH MARCH

from *The Ruins of Athens*

TRUMPET

By Ludwig van Beethoven

Moderately fast

TRACK 12

SYMPHONY NO. 9
Fourth Movement "Ode to Joy"

TRUMPET

By Ludwig van Beethoven

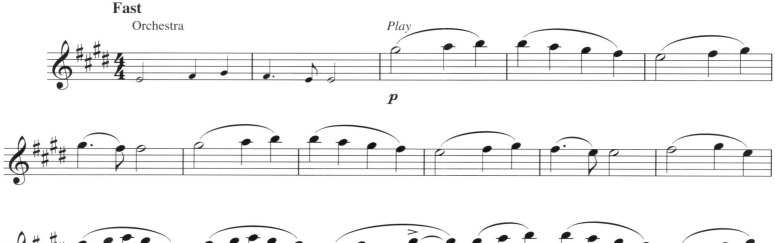

great songs series

This legendary series has delighted players and performers for generations.

Great Songs of Country Music

This volume features 58 country gems, including: Abilene • Afternoon Delight • Amazed • Annie's Song • Blue • Crazy • Elvira • Fly Away • For the Good Times • Friends in Low Places • The Gambler • Hey, Good Lookin' • I Hope You Dance • Thank God I'm a Country Boy • This Kiss • Your Cheatin' Heart • and more.
02500503 P/V/G......................................$19.95

Great Songs of Folk Music

Nearly 50 of the most popular folk songs of our time, including: Blowin' in the Wind • The House of the Rising Sun • Puff the Magic Dragon • This Land Is Your Land • Time in a Bottle • The Times They Are A-Changin' • The Unicorn • Where Have All the Flowers Gone? • and more.
02500997 P/V/G......................................$19.95

Great Songs from The Great American Songbook

52 American classics, including: Ain't That a Kick in the Head • As Time Goes By • Come Fly with Me •Georgia on My Mind • I Get a Kick Out of You • I've Got You Under My Skin • The Lady Is a Tramp • Love and Marriage • Mack the Knife • Misty • Over the Rainbow • People • Take the "A" Train • Thanks for the Memory • and more.
02500760 P/V/G......................................$16.95

Great Songs of the Movies

Nearly 60 of the best songs popularized in the movies, including: Accidentally in Love • Alfie • Almost Paradise • The Rainbow Connection • Somewhere in My Memory • Take My Breath Away (Love Theme) • Three Coins in the Fountain • (I've Had) the Time of My Life • Up Where We Belong • The Way We Were • and more.
02500967 P/V/G......................................$19.95

Great Songs of the Pop Era

Over 50 hits from the pop era, including: Every Breath You Take • I'm Every Woman • Just the Two of Us • Leaving on a Jet Plane • My Cherie Amour • Raindrops Keep Fallin' on My Head • Time After Time • (I've Had) the Time of My Life • What a Wonderful World • and more.
02500043 Easy Piano...........................$16.95

Great Songs of 2000-2009

Over 50 of the decade's biggest hits, including: Accidentally in Love • Breathe (2 AM) • Daughters • Hanging by a Moment • The Middle • The Remedy (I Won't Worry) • Smooth • A Thousand Miles • and more.
02500922 P/V/G......................................$24.99

Great Songs for Weddings

A beautiful collection of 59 pop standards perfect for wedding ceremonies and receptions, including: Always and Forever • Amazed • Beautiful in My Eyes • Can You Feel the Love Tonight • Endless Love • Love of a Lifetime • Open Arms • Unforgettable • When I Fall in Love • The Wind Beneath My Wings • and more.
02501006 P/V/G......................................$19.95

Great Songs of the Fifties

Features rock, pop, country, Broadway and movie tunes, including: All Shook Up • At the Hop • Blue Suede Shoes • Dream Lover • Fly Me to the Moon • Kansas City • Love Me Tender • Misty • Peggy Sue • Rock Around the Clock • Sea of Love • Sixteen Tons • Take the "A" Train • Wonderful! Wonderful! • and more. Includes an introduction by award-winning journalist Bruce Pollock.
02500323 P/V/G......................................$16.95

Great Songs of the Sixties, Vol. 1 – Revised

The updated version of this classic book includes 80 faves from the 1960s: Angel of the Morning • Bridge over Troubled Water • Cabaret • Different Drum • Do You Believe in Magic • Eve of Destruction • Monday, Monday • Spinning Wheel • Walk on By • and more.
02509902 P/V/G......................................$19.95

Great Songs of the Sixties, Vol. 2 – Revised

61 more '60s hits: California Dreamin' • Crying • For Once in My Life • Honey • Little Green Apples • MacArthur Park • Me and Bobby McGee • Nowhere Man • Piece of My Heart • Sugar, Sugar • You Made Me So Very Happy • and more.
02509904 P/V/G......................................$19.95

Great Songs of the Seventies, Vol. 1 – Revised

This super collection of 70 big hits from the '70s includes: After the Love Has Gone • Afternoon Delight • Annie's Song • Band on the Run • Cold as Ice • FM • Imagine • It's Too Late • Layla • Let It Be • Maggie May • Piano Man • Shelter from the Storm • Superstar • Sweet Baby James • Time in a Bottle • The Way We Were • and more.
02509917 P/V/G......................................$19.95

Great Songs of the Eighties – Revised

This edition features 50 songs in rock, pop & country styles, plus hits from Broadway and the movies! Songs: Almost Paradise • Angel of the Morning • Do You Really Want to Hurt Me • Endless Love • Flashdance...What a Feeling • Guilty • Hungry Eyes • (Just Like) Starting Over • Let Love Rule • Missing You • Patience • Through the Years • Time After Time • Total Eclipse of the Heart • and more.
02502125 P/V/G......................................$18.95

Great Songs of the Nineties

Includes: Achy Breaky Heart • Beautiful in My Eyes • Believe • Black Hole Sun • Black Velvet • Blaze of Glory • Building a Mystery • Crash into Me • Fields of Gold • From a Distance • Glycerine • Here and Now • Hold My Hand • I'll Make Love to You • Ironic • Linger • My Heart Will Go On • Waterfalls • Wonderwall • and more.
02500040 P/V/G......................................$16.95

Great Songs of Broadway

This fabulous collection of 60 standards includes: Getting to Know You • Hello, Dolly! • The Impossible Dream • Let Me Entertain You • My Favorite Things • My Husband Makes Movies • Oh, What a Beautiful Mornin' • On My Own • People • Tomorrow • Try to Remember • Unusual Way • What I Did for Love • and dozens more, plus an introductory article.
02500615 P/V/G......................................$19.95

Great Songs for Children

90 wonderful, singable favorites kids love: Baa Baa Black Sheep • Bingo • The Candy Man • Do-Re-Mi • Eensy Weensy Spider • The Hokey Pokey • Linus and Lucy • Sing • This Old Man • Yellow Submarine • and more, with a touching foreword by Grammy-winning singer/songwriter Tom Chapin.
02501348 P/V/G......................................$19.99

Great Songs of Classic Rock

Nearly 50 of the greatest songs of the rock era, including: Against the Wind • Cold As Ice • Don't Stop Believin' • Feels like the First Time • I Can See for Miles • Maybe I'm Amazed • Minute by Minute • Money • Nights in White Satin • Only the Lonely • Open Arms • Rikki Don't Lose That Number • Rosanna • We Are the Champions • and more.
02500801 P/V/G......................................$19.95

Prices, contents, and availability subject to change without notice.

More Great Piano/Vocal Books

FROM CHERRY LANE

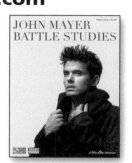

For a complete listing of Cherry Lane titles available, including contents listings, please visit our web site at
www.cherrylane.com

02501136	Sara Bareilles – Little Voice	$16.95
02502171	The Best of Boston	$17.95
02501123	Buffy the Vampire Slayer – Once More with Feeling	$18.95
02500665	Sammy Cahn Songbook	$24.95
02501454	Colbie Caillat – Breakthrough	$17.99
02501127	Colbie Caillat – Coco	$16.95
02500144	Mary Chapin Carpenter – Party Doll & Other Favorites	$16.95
02502165	John Denver Anthology – Revised	$22.95
02500002	John Denver Christmas	$14.95
02502166	John Denver's Greatest Hits	$17.95
02502151	John Denver – A Legacy in Song (Softcover)	$24.95
02502152	John Denver – A Legacy in Song (Hardcover)	$34.95
02500566	Poems, Prayers and Promises: The Art and Soul of John Denver	$19.95
02500326	John Denver – The Wildlife Concert	$17.95
02500501	John Denver and the Muppets: A Christmas Together	$9.95
02501186	The Dresden Dolls – The Virginia Companion	$39.95
02509922	The Songs of Bob Dylan	$29.95
02500586	Linda Eder – Broadway My Way	$14.95
02500497	Linda Eder – Gold	$14.95
02500396	Linda Eder – Christmas Stays the Same	$17.95
02500175	Linda Eder – It's No Secret Anymore	$14.95
02502209	Linda Eder – It's Time	$17.95
02500630	Donald Fagen – 5 of the Best	$7.95
02500535	Erroll Garner Anthology	$19.95
02500318	Gladiator	$12.95
02502126	Best of Guns N' Roses	$17.95
02502072	Guns N' Roses – Selections from Use Your Illusion I and II	$17.95
02500014	Sir Roland Hanna Collection	$19.95
02500856	Jack Johnson – Anthology	$19.95
02501140	Jack Johnson – Sleep Through the Static	$16.95
02500381	Lenny Kravitz – Greatest Hits	$14.95
02501318	John Legend – Evolver	$19.99

02503701	Man of La Mancha	$11.95
02501047	Dave Matthews Band – Anthology	$24.95
02500693	Dave Matthews – Some Devil	$16.95
02500493	Dave Matthews Band – Live in Chicago 12/19/98 at the United Center	$14.95
02502192	Dave Matthews Band – Under the Table and Dreaming	$17.95
02501504	John Mayer – Battle Studies	$19.99
02500987	John Mayer – Continuum	$16.95
02500681	John Mayer – Heavier Things	$16.95
02500563	John Mayer – Room for Squares	$16.95
02500081	Natalie Merchant – Ophelia	$14.95
02500863	Jason Mraz – Mr. A-Z	$17.95
02501467	Jason Mraz – We Sing. We Dance. We Steal Things.	$19.99
02502895	Nine	$17.95
02500425	Time and Love: The Art and Soul of Laura Nyro	$21.95
02502204	The Best of Metallica	$17.95
02501336	Amanda Palmer – Who Killed Amanda Palmer?	$17.99
02501004	Best of Gram Parsons	$16.95
02501137	Tom Paxton – Comedians & Angels	$16.95
02500010	Tom Paxton – The Honor of Your Company	$17.95
02507962	Peter, Paul & Mary – Holiday Concert	$17.95
02500145	Pokemon 2.B.A. Master	$12.95
02500026	The Prince of Egypt	$16.95
02500660	Best of Bonnie Raitt	$17.95
02502189	The Bonnie Raitt Collection	$22.95
02502088	Bonnie Raitt – Luck of the Draw	$14.95
02507958	Bonnie Raitt – Nick of Time	$14.95
02502218	Kenny Rogers – The Gift	$16.95
02500414	Shrek	$16.99
02500536	Spirit – Stallion of the Cimarron	$16.95
02500166	Steely Dan – Anthology	$17.95
02500622	Steely Dan – Everything Must Go	$14.95
02500284	Steely Dan – Two Against Nature	$14.95
02500344	Billy Strayhorn: An American Master	$17.95
02502132	Barbra Streisand – Back to Broadway	$19.95

02500515	Barbra Streisand – Christmas Memories	$16.95
02507969	Barbra Streisand – A Collection: Greatest Hits and More	$17.95
02502164	Barbra Streisand – The Concert	$22.95
02500550	Essential Barbra Streisand	$24.95
02502228	Barbra Streisand – Higher Ground	$16.95
02501065	Barbra Streisand – Live in Concert 2006	$19.95
02500196	Barbra Streisand – A Love Like Ours	$16.95
02503617	John Tesh – Avalon	$15.95
02502178	The John Tesh Collection	$17.95
02503623	John Tesh – A Family Christmas	$15.95
02503630	John Tesh – Grand Passion	$16.95
02500307	John Tesh – Pure Movies 2	$16.95
02501068	The Evolution of Robin Thicke	$19.95
02500565	Thoroughly Modern Millie	$17.99
02501399	Best of Toto	$19.99
02500576	Toto – 5 of the Best	$7.95
02502175	Tower of Power – Silver Anniversary	$17.95
02501403	Keith Urban – Defying Gravity	$17.99
02501008	Keith Urban – Love, Pain & The Whole Crazy Thing	$17.95
02501141	Keith Urban – Greatest Hits	$16.99
02502198	The "Weird Al" Yankovic Anthology	$17.95
02502217	Trisha Yearwood – A Collection of Hits	$16.95
02500334	Maury Yeston – December Songs	$17.95
02502225	The Maury Yeston Songbook	$19.95

See your local music dealer or contact:

Cherry Lane music company

EXCLUSIVELY DISTRIBUTED BY
HAL•LEONARD® CORPORATION
7777 W. BLUEMOUND RD. P.O. BOX 13819 MILWAUKEE, WI 53213

Prices, contents and availability subject to change without notice.

0310